X-TREME FACTS: CONTINENTS

AFRICA

by Catherine C. Finan

BEARPORT
PUBLISHING

Minneapolis, Minnesota

Credits:

Title Page, Graeme Shannon/Shutterstock; 4–5, Galyna Andrushko/Shutterstock; 4 top left, Anna Om/Shutterstock; 4 top middle, Brocreative/Shutterstock; 4 top right, Peter Hermes Furian/Shutterstock; 4 bottom, Viacheslav Lopatin/Shutterstock; 5 top, UNESCO/Creative Commons; 5 top left, 8 left, 13 top right, 21 top left, LightField Studios/Shutterstock; 5 top middle, Mike Peel/Creative Commons; 5 middle, Pecold/Shutterstock.com; 5 bottm left, Catmando/Shutterstock; 5 bottom middle, GTS Productions/Shutterstock.com; 5 bottom right, PixHound/Shutterstock; 6 top, TOP67/Shutterstock; 6, VaniaWidyaya/Shutterstock; 6 bottom left, AY Amazefoto/Shutterstock.com; 6 bottom middle left, Kues/Shutterstock; 6 bottom middle right, Kues/Shutterstock; 6 bottom right, Katiekk/Shutterstock.com; 7 top, Jahidul-hasan/Shutterstock.com; 7 middle, Oleg Znamenskiy/Shutterstock; 7 bottom, Mieszko9/Shutterstock; 7 bottom right, Aleksandar Todorovic/Shutterstock.com; 8–9, givaga/Shutterstock; 8 top right, Shannon1/Creative Commons; 8, Sarine Arslanian/Shutterstock.com; 8 middle, Prostock-studio/Shutterstock; 9 top, Bionet/Public Domain; 9 top right, Albert Kretschmer/Public Domain; 9 middle, Valentina Razumova/Shutterstock; 9 bottom, Ahmed.campa4412/Creative Commons; 9 bottom left, Elenarts/Shutterstock; 9 bottom right, Frederick Arthur Bridgman/Public Domain; 10 top, Jack Barker/ Alamy Stock Photo; 10, Sjoerdug/Creative Commons; 10 bottom left, Jeka/Shutterstock; 10 bottom right, Tykhanskyi Viacheslav/Shutterstock; 11 top, Manfidza/Creative Commons; 11 top left, Nanette Dreyer/Shutterstock; 11 middle, cdrin/Shutterstock; 11 bottom, Radek Borovka/Shutterstock; 12 top, Chipdawes/Public Domain; 12, Marcella Miriello/Shutterstock; 12 left, Eric Isselee/Shutterstock; 13 top, Guenter Albers/Shutterstock; 13 top left, Ttatty/Shutterstock.com; 13 bottom, evenfh/Shutterstock; 13 bottom right, Public Domain; 14, KATERINA_2503/Shutterstock; 14 left, Jen Watson/Shutterstock; 15 top, Claude Huot/Shutterstock; 15 top right, engagestock/Shutterstock; 15 middle Svetlana Foote/Shutterstock; 15 bottom, Volodymyr Burdiak/Shutterstock; 15 bottom right, Villiers Steyn/Shutterstock; 16–17, EastVillage Images/Shutterstock; 17 top, GUDKOV ANDREY/Shutterstock; 17 top right, Jose Angel Astor Rocha/Shutterstock; 17 middle, Danita Delimont/Shutterstock; 17 bottom, Henk Bogaard/Shutterstock; 17 bottom left, Rikus Visser/Shutterstock; 17 bottom middle, Kanokratnok/Shutterstock.com; 18 top, sasimoto/Shutterstock; 18 middle, cpaulfell/Shutterstock; 18 bottom, Oleg Znamenskiy/Shutterstock; 19 top, FCG/Shutterstock; 19 top right, AVRORACOON/Shutterstock; 19 middle, WitR/Shutterstock; 19 bottom, Volodymyr Burdiak/Shutterstock; 19 bottom left, Maridav/Shutterstock; 20 top, ArCaLu/Shutterstock; 20 bottom, Christoph Hormann/Creative Commons; 20 bottom left, nortongo/Shutterstock; 20 bottom right, MOIZ HUSEIN STORYTELLER/Shutterstock.com; 21 top, Neander-thal-Museum, Mettmann/Creative Commons; 21 top left, Johannes Maximilian at Wikimedia Commons, GFDL 1.2; 21 bottom, Syllabub/Creative Commons; 21 bottom center, Avinash Deo/Shutterstock; 22 top, Nupo Deyon Daniel/Creative Commons; 22 top left, fizkes/Shutterstock; 22 top right, Jordi C/Shutterstock.com; 22 bottom, givaga/Shutterstock; 23 top right, Delpixel/Shutterstock; 23 top, Boris Macek/Creative Commons; 23 middle, NJR ZA/Creative Commons; 23 bottom, Diego Delso/Creative Commons; 23 bottom right, Mark Fisher/Shutterstock.com; 24 top right, grafvision/Shutterstock; 24 top, Media Lens King/Shutterstock; 24 top left, Roman Samborskyi/Shutterstock; 24 bottom left, dwi putra stock/Shutterstock; 24 bottom right, Ranta Images/Shutterstock; 25 top, i_am_zews/Shutterstock; 25 top left, CGN089/Shutterstock; 25 middle left, Kenyan nature/Shutterstock; 25 middle right, Creative Commons; 25 bottom, Sunshine Seeds/Shutterstock.com; 25 bottom right, paffy/Shutterstock; 26 top, abdozaghloul/Shutterstock; 26, Erica Lorimer Images/Shutterstock.com; 27 top, Ossewa/Creative Commons; 27 middle, Odua Images/Shutterstock; 27 bottom, Wirestock Creators/ Shutterstock.com; 28 top, Minal Jain/Shutterstock; 28 bottom, Tanawit Sabprasan/Shutterstock; 28-29, Austen Photography

Bearport Publishing Company Product Development Team

President: Jen Jenson; Director of Product Development: Spencer Brinker; Managing Editor: Allison Juda; Associate Editor: Naomi Reich; Associate Editor: Tiana Tran; Art Director: Colin O'Dea; Designer: Elena Klinkner; Designer: Kayla Eggert; Product Development Assistant: Owen Hamlin

Produced for Bearport Publishing by BlueAppleWorks Inc.
Managing Editor for BlueAppleWorks: Melissa McClellan
Art Director: T.J. Choleva
Photo Research: Jane Reid

STATEMENT ON USAGE OF GENERATIVE ARTIFICIAL INTELLIGENCE
Bearport Publishing remains committed to publishing high-quality nonfiction books. Therefore, we restrict the use of generative AI to ensure accuracy of all text and visual components pertaining to a book's subject. See BearportPublishing.com for details.

Library of Congress Cataloging-in-Publication Data

Names: Finan, Catherine C., 1972- author.
Title: Africa / by Catherine C. Finan.
Other titles: X-treme facts: Continents.
Description: Minneapolis, Minnesota : Bearport Publishing Company, [2024] |
    Series: X-treme facts: Continents | Includes bibliographical references
    and index.
Identifiers: LCCN 2023030962 (print) | LCCN 2023030963 (ebook) | ISBN
    9798889164302 (library binding) | ISBN 9798889164388 (paperback) | ISBN
    9798889164456 (ebook)
Subjects: LCSH: Africa--Juvenile literature.
Classification: LCC DT3 .F49 2024 (print) | LCC DT3 (ebook) | DDC
    960--dcundefined
LC record available at https://lccn.loc.gov/2023030962
LC ebook record available at https://lccn.loc.gov/2023030963

Copyright © 2024 Bearport Publishing Company. All rights reserved. No part of this publication may be reproduced in whole or in part, stored in any retrieval system, or transmitted in any form or by any means, electronic, mechanical, photocopying, recording, or otherwise, without written permission from the publisher.

For more information, write to Bearport Publishing, 5357 Penn Avenue South, Minneapolis, MN 55419.

Contents

The Mother Continent ... 4

Now That's Hot! ... 6

The Nifty Nile ... 8

More Wonderful Water ... 10

Plenty of Pyramids ... 12

African Animal Adventure ... 14

Across the Serengeti ... 16

A Land of Contrasts ... 18

The Great Divide ... 20

See You in the City! ... 22

Taste of the Cultures ... 24

Amazing Africa ... 26

Make a Mbira ... 28

Glossary ... 30

Read More ... 31

Learn More Online ... 31

Index ... 32

About the Author ... 32

The Mother Continent

Where on Earth have people lived for the longest? Africa! This **continent** was home to humans' earliest **ancestors**. That's how it got its nickname—the Mother Continent. Africa is the world's second-largest continent and is made up of an incredible 54 countries. It has **habitats** ranging from hot deserts and open grasslands to lush rainforests and snow-capped mountains. Let's explore this amazing continent!

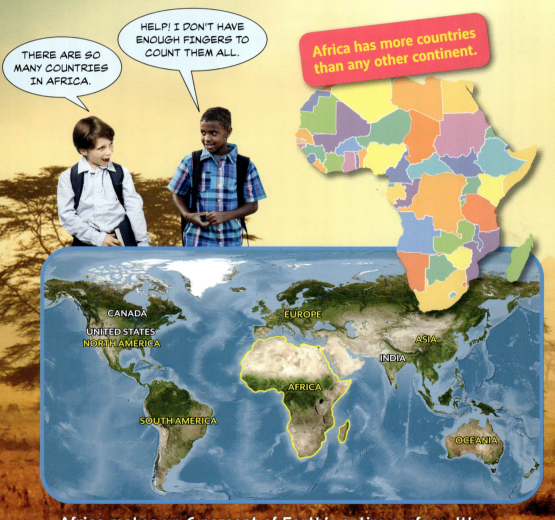

Africa makes up 6 percent of Earth's entire surface. It's larger than the United States, Canada, and India put together.

Africa is also called the cradle of humankind. It's the only place where we've found **fossil** records of human ancestors that stretch through millions of years.

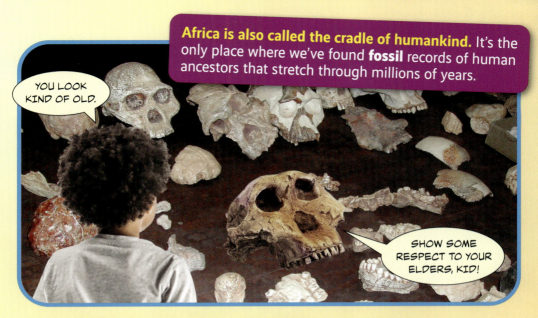

YOU LOOK KIND OF OLD.

SHOW SOME RESPECT TO YOUR ELDERS, KID!

Humans and our ancestors have lived in Africa for more than four million years!

Africa's population is about **1.3 billion people.**

More than 2,000 different languages are spoken in Africa.

The word *Africa* may come from the Egyptian word *Afru-ika*, which means motherland, or the Latin word *aprica*, meaning sunny.

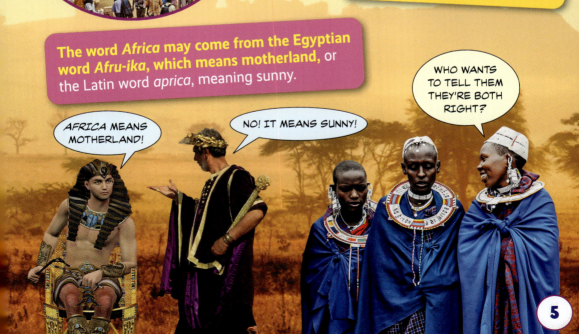

AFRICA MEANS MOTHERLAND!

NO! IT MEANS SUNNY!

WHO WANTS TO TELL THEM THEY'RE BOTH RIGHT?

5

Now That's Hot!

In addition to being large, much of Africa is hot! In fact, Africa is Earth's hottest continent. Much of the northern part of Africa is covered by the Sahara—the world's largest hot desert. During summer, the Sahara's average daytime temperature is a sizzling 104 degrees Fahrenheit (40 degrees Celsius), but it's often even hotter. The hottest temperature ever recorded in the Sahara was a whopping 125°F (51°C). It's hard to beat that heat!

Blowing winds in the Sahara form sand **dunes** that can be more than 1,000 feet (300 m) high. That's about as tall as the Eiffel Tower!

The Sahara is dry. A large part of the desert gets less than 1 inch (3 cm) of rain a year.

FINGERS CROSSED IT DOESN'T RAIN!

BUT YOU WILL NEED A WARM JACKET AT NIGHT!

SILLY TOURISTS! YOU DON'T NEED AN UMBRELLA HERE!

Visit the desert after the sun goes down, and the Sahara is very different. **At night, temperatures can drop to a chilly 21°F (−6°C).** *Brrrrr!*

People often ride camels to cross the Sahara. These animals store fat in their humps and can go days without food or water.

The continent has many hot deserts. **The Kalahari in the south is Africa's second-largest desert.**

In the desert, people often dress in loose-fitting clothes to keep cool. Head coverings protect against sunburn and blowing sand.

The Nifty Nile

Part of one of Earth's longest rivers runs through the super-dry Sahara. Almost 1,000 miles (1,600 km) of the Nile River flows through the hot sand and provides much-needed water to the people who live close by. In fact, people have lived along and relied upon the Nile for thousands of years. Starting about 5,000 years ago, ancient Egypt grew up around the river. It's time to find out what makes the Nile so nifty!

The Nile starts near Lake Victoria in Uganda. **The river flows north—one of the few rivers to do so!**

LET'S FOLLOW THE NILE ALL THE WAY TO EGYPT!

SERIOUSLY? IT WILL BE A LONG WAY NORTH!

The Nile is about 4,130 miles (6,650 km) long and flows through 11 countries, including Egypt. Today, 95 percent of Egypt's population still lives near it!

Many say the Nile is Earth's longest river. Others think it's the Amazon in South America. Disagreement about where each river starts leaves things up for debate.

Ancient Egyptians relied on the Nile's yearly flooding to provide rich soil along the riverbank for farming.

Your bed sheets might be made from cotton grown along the Nile! **This cotton is known for its excellent quality.**

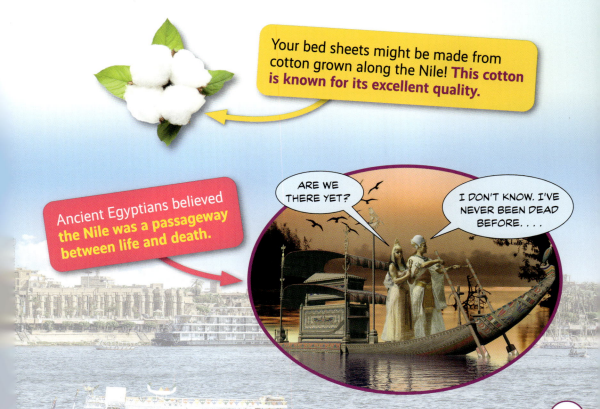

Ancient Egyptians believed **the Nile was a passageway between life and death.**

More Wonderful Water

The Nile might be the most well-known, but there are many other wonderful water features across Africa. Not only is Lake Victoria thought to be the source of the Nile, it's also Earth's second-largest freshwater lake. Another spectacular sight is Victoria Falls. Stretching more than 5,500 ft (1,700 m) along the border of Zambia and Zimbabwe, it's Earth's widest waterfall and one of the Seven Natural Wonders of the World.

Lake Victoria has about 1,000 islands. On Mfangano Island, there are ancient cave paintings made by the Twa people more than 2,000 years ago.

Lake Victoria looks more like a sea than a lake. Its coastline is more than 2,000 miles (3,200 km) long.

IT'S GOING TO TAKE FOREVER TO GET ACROSS THIS LAKE.

WELL, YEAH. MAYBE RAISE THE SAIL TO SPEED IT UP!

Up to 132 million gallons (500 million L) of water plunge over Victoria Falls every minute. That's enough water to fill 200 Olympic-sized swimming pools.

Lake Malawi is another incredible body of water. It has more **species** of fish than any other lake on Earth!

Plenty of Pyramids

Alongside the incredible waters of Africa you can find amazing things humans built long ago. Just look at the **pyramids**! Many of ancient Egypt's pyramids can be found near the end of the Nile. The most famous are in the city of Giza. These huge structures were built about 4,500 years ago as tombs for Egyptian **pharaohs**. And Egypt isn't the only country in Africa with pyramids—Sudan has about twice as many!

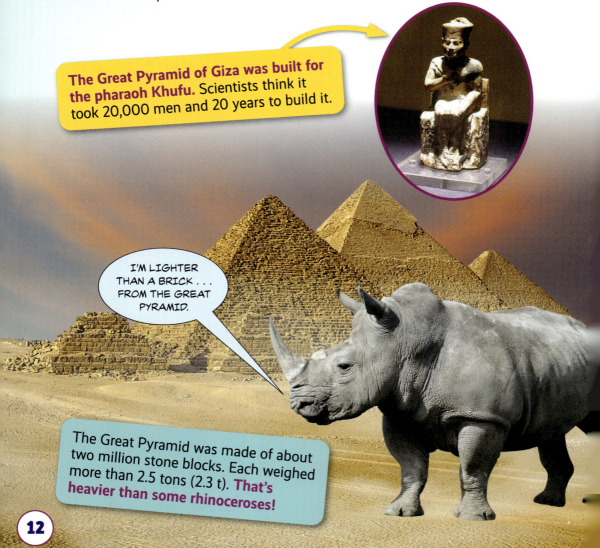

The Great Pyramid of Giza was built for the pharaoh Khufu. Scientists think it took 20,000 men and 20 years to build it.

I'M LIGHTER THAN A BRICK . . . FROM THE GREAT PYRAMID.

The Great Pyramid was made of about two million stone blocks. Each weighed more than 2.5 tons (2.3 t). **That's heavier than some rhinoceroses!**

Although pharaohs were **mummified**, no mummies have been found at Giza. Robbers stole them hundreds of years ago.

Treasure hunter Giuseppe Ferlini is thought to have raided and destroyed more than 40 of Sudan's pyramids in the 1830s.

African Animal Adventure

If you think pointed pyramids are impressive, check out Africa's amazing animals. The continent is home to some of Earth's largest, tallest, fastest, and deadliest animals. People travel from all over the world to experience this wonderful wildlife. What are some of the most awesome animals that call Africa home?

Giraffes win the record for tallest land animal. They grow to be 18 ft (6 m) tall. That's taller than three adult humans standing on one another's shoulders.

African elephants, Earth's largest land animals, can live for about 70 years. **They have 150,000 different bundles of muscles in their trunks alone!**

Believe it or not, the hippo is Africa's deadliest animal. About 500 people are killed by hippos every year.

Across the Serengeti

When it comes to spotting the continent's wildlife, the Serengeti is one of the best places to be. This huge **plain** in east Africa is where you'll catch the Great **Migration** each year. From July to October, millions of animals cross from Tanzania's Serengeti National Park to Kenya's Masai Mara National Reserve in search of food and water. But it's a dangerous trip. The animals are followed by predators, and many don't survive the journey.

More than 1.5 million wildebeests attempt the migration.

Thousands of zebras and gazelles make the migration, too.

About 250,000 wildebeests die during migration. Those that aren't killed by predators may starve to death or drown while crossing rivers.

A Land of Contrasts

From grassy plains to barren deserts, Africa is a land of wonder. If you traveled the continent from west to east and north to south, you'd see many habitats and landforms. The Sahara stretches across northern Africa, then it gives way to the wildlife-rich grasslands of the **savanna**, which covers nearly half the continent. Central Africa features Earth's second-largest tropical forest. And then there's Tanzania's Mount Kilimanjaro, Africa's highest peak. What a view!

Sharp thorns protect the savanna's acacia trees from many leaf-eating animals. However, a giraffe's long, flexible tongue can still get to the tasty leaves.

HA! YOUR THORNS WON'T STOP ME!

The Namib Desert is a cold desert along Africa's southwestern coast. In some areas, pools of salt water have **evaporated**, leaving behind only the salt.

Central Africa's rain forest is home to many **primates**, including monkeys, chimpanzees, and gorillas. **Elephants and antelope also live there.**

The tall trees in Africa's rainforest block sunlight from reaching the forest floor. Here, creepy-crawly termites and slugs eat dead bits of trees.

Motlatse Canyon in South Africa is the world's third-largest canyon.

Mount Kilimanjaro is Earth's highest stand-alone mountain. It rises more than 19,000 ft (5,900 m) above the surrounding land.

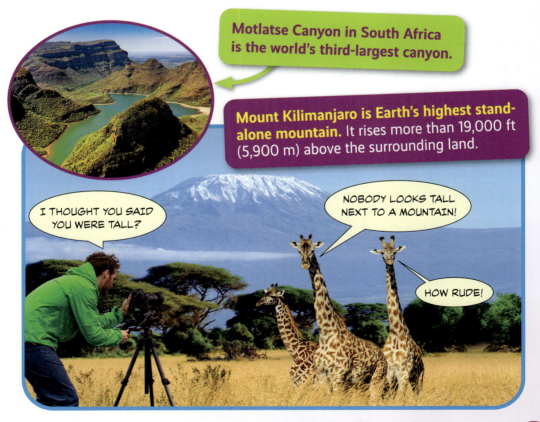

A South African man named Bernard Goosen scaled the famous mountain twice—in a wheelchair!

The Great Divide

Any conversation about the continent's landforms would be incomplete without mentioning the Great Rift Valley. Found mostly in east Africa, this vast break in Earth's surface stretches on for 4,000 miles (6,400 km). The valley sits on two large plates in Earth's crust. Over millions of years, these sections spread apart, creating a place with dramatic views for unique animal life and some of our earliest human ancestors!

On average, the valley is about 40 miles (60 km) wide. At its widest, it stretches 300 miles (480 km) across.

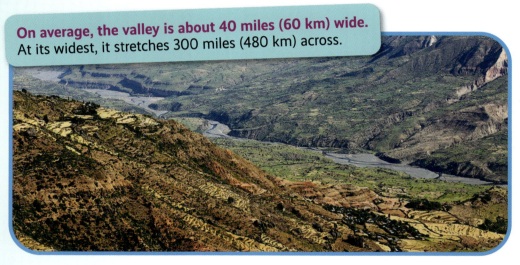

Steep cliffs tower some 3,000 ft (900 m) above the valley floor. Some soar to 9,000 ft (2,700 m) tall.

Today, scientists studying the movement of Earth's plates in the valley believe **Africa will split into two pieces over the next millions of years.**

DO YOU WORRY ABOUT AFRICA SPLITTING APART?

NOT REALLY. IT'S BEEN SPLITTING FOR AGES!

The bones were discovered to be from a female. She was given the name Lucy.

See You in the City!

In Africa's many spectacular cities, you'll find a variety of cultures that make the continent so unique. Many cities are huge and modern. Others are smaller coastal spots known for their natural beauty. From busy streets and soaring skyscrapers to sunny beaches and colorful spice markets, Africa's cities deserve a grand tour!

Lagos, Nigeria, is Africa's largest city. By 2100 it's expected to be the world's largest city, with a population of 90 million.

Cairo, Egypt, is Africa's second-largest city. About 21 million people call it home.

You can visit a blue city in northwest Morocco. **The city of Chefchaouen is painted in beautiful shades of blue!**

Wander through the colorful spice markets in Marrakech, Morocco. In addition to spices, the sellers have hand-woven baskets, hats, rugs, and more!

One of Africa's tallest buildings is Hillbrow Tower in Johannesburg, South Africa. At almost 890 ft (270 m) high, it's about as tall as 50 giraffes stacked.

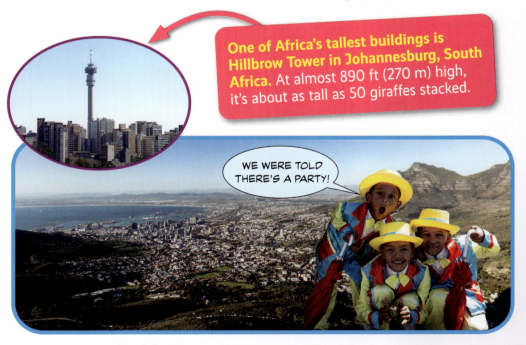

WE WERE TOLD THERE'S A PARTY!

One of Africa's southernmost cities is Cape Town, South Africa. The city has many festivals throughout the year celebrating African culture and creativity.

Taste of the Cultures

After visiting Africa's cities, you might be hungry. It's a good thing there is amazing food all across the continent! Thanks to the many different climates, a variety of crops grow here. From peanuts, cassava, and plantains to corn, coconuts, and a lot of spices, Africa is bursting with flavor! For many African cultures, eating is a way to bring people together. So, grab a plate and explore some yummy dishes!

Most of Africa's cacao beans grow in Ivory Coast, Ghana, Nigeria, and Cameroon. Ivory Coast alone produces 40 percent of the world's supply.

I DON'T SEE ANY CACAO BEANS!

OH, THE GOOD STUFF IS HIDING INSIDE.

WHAT'S IN THIS COFFEE?

I'M NOT SURE YOU WANT TO KNOW. . . .

Kopi luwak is made from coffee beans found in the poop of catlike creatures called civets. Would you try it?

24

YOU HAVE ENOUGH PLANTAINS HERE FOR A WHOLE VILLAGE.

DON'T BE SILLY. WE HAVE ENOUGH FOR THE WHOLE WORLD!

Uganda grows the most plantains of any country in the world. This type of banana can be used in both sweet and **savory** dishes.

Although there are many different cultures, some dishes are found all over. A thick porridge made from cornmeal is cooked throughout Africa and has many different names.

IT'S BRAAI, NOT BARBECUE!

I FEEL LIKE WE'VE BEEN HERE FOREVER. . . .

In South Africa, a braai is a way to roast meat over a fire. It's also a gathering with family and friends that can last for hours!

25

Amazing Africa

You could spend a lifetime exploring Africa's magnificent wonders! The continent's sprawling deserts, lush jungles, and sun-soaked plains are a beautiful backdrop to some of Earth's most incredible wildlife—and the start of all of humankind. From its ancient pyramids to its modern bustling cities, Africa is sure to delight. What amazing things will you explore?

In Fez, Morocco, the world's oldest continually operating university—the University of Al-Karaouine—was founded in 859 CE!

The average age of Africa's people is younger than on any other continent.

By 2050, Africa's population will likely double to about 2.4 billion people! That means a quarter of all people on Earth will be African.

26

In South Africa, you can find the highest bridge bungee jump in the world at Bloukrans Bridge. Would you take the leap?

Rwanda was one of the first countries in the world to ban plastic bags.

Make a Mbira

Craft Project

Across Africa, many important events—such as birthday celebrations and weddings—have music. Popular instruments include the xylophone, drums, shakers, and rattles. But let's not forget the mbira, otherwise known as the thumb piano. Make your own mbira, and get the party started!

The mbira was being played about 1,300 years ago in what is now Mali and Zimbabwe.

What You Will Need

- A piece of cardboard 3¾ x 4½ in. (9 x 12 cm)
- Markers or crayons
- 4 craft sticks
- 2 rubber bands
- 4 bobby pins

The wooden instrument can be hollow or solid. The keys are made from metal.

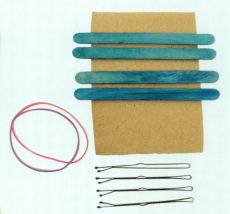

Step One

Decorate the cardboard with markers or crayons.

Step Two

Stack two craft sticks on top of the cardboard and two underneath in the same spot at one end of the cardboard.

Step Three

Tightly wrap a rubber band around the craft sticks on each side of the cardboard.

Step Four

Open a bobby pin a little and push the bottom part of the pin under the top two craft sticks. Repeat with the other three bobby pins. Now, you are ready to play the mbira!

ancestors members of a family or group who lived a long time ago

continent one of Earth's seven large land masses

dunes large mounds of sand in a desert

evaporated changed from a liquid into a gas

fossil the remains of a plant or animal from long ago that has turned to rock

habitats the natural environments of animals or plants

migration the movement of animals from one place to another at a certain time of the year

mummified preserved by drying out the body and wrapping it tightly with cloth

oases areas in a desert where there is water and where people can live and raise crops

pharaohs rulers of ancient Egypt

plain a large, flat area of land

primates members of the group of animals that include humans, monkeys, and apes

pyramids stone structures with square bases and triangular sides that meet at a point on top

savanna a flat plain covered in grass and with few trees

savory flavor that is spicy or salty but not sweet or bitter

species groups that living things are divided into according to similar characteristics

symbolize to represent something else

Read More

Aspen-Baxter, Linda. *Africa (Exploring Continents).* New York: Lightbox Learning Inc., 2023.

Finan, Catherine C. *Ancient Egypt (X-Treme Facts: Ancient History).* Minneapolis: Bearport Publishing Company, 2022.

Vonder Brink, Tracy. *Africa (Seven Continents of the World).* New York: Crabtree Publishing Company, 2023.

Learn More Online

1. Go to **www.factsurfer.com** or scan the QR code below.

2. Enter **"X-treme Africa"** into the search box.

3. Click on the cover of this book to see a list of websites.

Index

ancient Egypt 8–9, 12
cacao beans 24
Egypt 8, 12, 22
Giza 12–13
Great Migration 16
Great Rift Valley 20–21
human ancestors 4–5, 20–21
Kenya 10, 16
Lake Victoria 8, 10
Maasai people 17
Masai Mara National Reserve 16
Morocco 23, 26
Mount Kilimanjaro 18–19
Nigeria 22, 24
Nile River 8–10, 12
population 5, 8, 21–22, 26
pyramids 12–14, 22, 26
rainforest 4, 19
Sahara 6–8, 11, 18
savanna 18
Serengeti National Park 16–17
South Africa 19, 23, 25, 27
Victoria Falls 10–11

About the Author

Catherine C. Finan is a writer living in northeastern Pennsylvania. One of her most memorable experiences was riding a camel in Essaouira, Morocco.